La Alhambra

An Arab dream in Europe

By Carolina Mazon

La Alhambra

An Arab dream in Europe

By Carolina Mazon

La Alhambra is an Arab fortress sited in Granada, in the south of Spain, that was the final residence of the last Arab king in Europe. He was expelled from Spain by the so named "catholic kings" Elizabeth of Castille and Ferdinand of Aragon, in the very same year as America was discovered by Columbus (1492).

Being not far from Sierra Nevada, nowadays it has become a popular destiny to ski and go afterwards to the coast of Granada to take a swim.

Note: the Muslim religion does not allow to portray representations of living beings, therefore La Alhambra is mostly decorated with passages from poets carved on the stone walls. You will find the translation of some of these excerpts in this book.

Author: Carolina Mazon, Spain

ISBN: 978-1-71661-692-1

2020 - All rights reserved

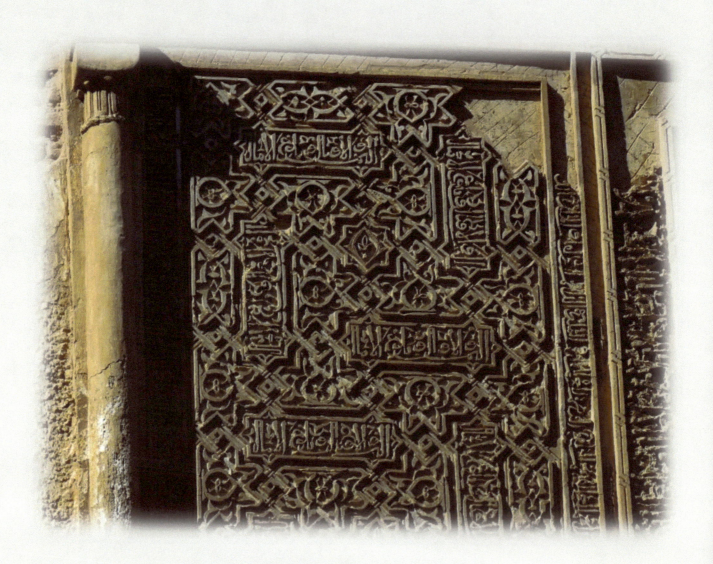

«This piece of art has come to decorate the Alhambra; which is the home of the peaceful and of the warriors; Calahorra that contains a palace. ¡Say that it is at the same time a fortress and a mansion for joy! It is a palace in which magnificence is shared among its ceiling, its floor and its four walls; on the stuccowork and on the glazed tiles there are wonders, but the carved wooden ceilings are even more extraordinary; these were all united and their union gave birth to the most perfect construction in the place where the highest mansion already stood; they seem poetic images, paronomasias and transpositions, the decorative branches and inlays. Yusuf's visage appears before us as a sign that is where all the perfections have met. It is from the glorious tribe of Jazray, whose works in favour of the religion are like dawn, when its light appears in the horizon.»

«I am a crown on the front of my door: in me is the West envious of the East. Al-Gani billah orders me to quickly give way to the victory, as soon as it calls. I am always waiting to see the visage of the king, dawn appearing from the horizon. May God make his works as beautiful as are his mettle and his figure!»

«May the One who granted the imam Mohammed with the beautiful ideas to decorate his mansions be blessed. For, are there not in this garden wonders that God has made incomparable in their beauty, and a sculpture of pearls with a transparently light, the borders of which are trimmed with seed pearl?

Melted silver flows through the pearls, to which it resembles in its pure dawn beauty.

Apparently, water and marble seem to be one, without letting us know which of them is flowing.

Don't you see how the water spills on the basin, but its spouts hide it immediately?

It is a lover whose eyelids are brimming over with tears, tears that it hides from fear of a betrayer.

Isn't it, in fact, like a white cloud that pours its water channels on the lions and seems the hand of the caliph, who, in the morning, grants the war lions with his favors?

Those who gaze at the lions in a threatening attitude, (knows that) only respect (to the Emir) holds his anger.

Oh descendant of the Ansares, and not through an indirect line, heritage of nobility, who despises the fatuous: May the peace of God be with you and may your life be long and unscathed multiplying your feasts and tormenting your enemies!»

Translation by www.alhambradegranada.org

«I am a water orb that appears before the creatures limpid and transparent a great Ocean, the shores of which are select pieces of work made of special marble and the waters of which, shaped like pearls, flow on an enormous sheet of ice that has been delicately carved. In occasions I am overflowed with water, but I, from time to time, part with the transparent veil that covers me. Then I and that part of the water that comes from the borders of the fountain, appear like a piece of ice, part of which melts, and the rest does not. But, when rivers flow, we are only comparable to star-studded sky. I am also a mother-of-pearl and the pearls are the drops, similar to the jewelry of the right hand that an artisan placed on Ibn Nasr's crown, who, for me, was generous with the treasures of his fortune. May he live with double happiness, he, who up to the date has been the thoughtful man of the lineage of Galib, of the children of prosperity, of the fortunate ones, stars shining goodness, delicate noble mansion. Of the children of the tribe of the Jazray, of those who proclaimed the truth and protected the Prophet. He has been the new Sa'd who, with his banns, has dispelled all the darkness and turned it into light and he has given prosperity to his vassals by creating a stable peace in the surrounding areas. He placed the throne as a guarantee of security for the religion and the believers. And he has granted me the highest degree of beauty, so that my shape causes the admiration of the sages. For never have any eyes seen a greater thing than myself, neither in the East nor in the West and in no time has any king, neither abroad nor in Arabia, achieved anything similar to me.»

«Taca on the door of the happiest hall to serve His Highness in the mirador.

¡My God, how beautiful it is when hold by the right hand of the incomparable king!

When glasses of water appear on it, they are like maidens above.

Rejoice at Ismail, thanks to whom God has honored you and made you happy.

¡May the Islam subsist thanks to him so strongly, that it will be the defense of the throne! »

Printed in the USA
CPSIA information can be obtained
at www.ICGtesting.com
LVHW062311191124
797115LV00012B/121